Sticker Fun

Puppies
and Dogs

ARMADILLO

Little dogs

Which is the most adorable little dog?

three fluffy
poodles

floppy eared
spaniel

dear little
dachshund

cute little corgi

bright eyed
beagle

cuddly corgi

I might be little,
but I'm bigger
than you!

happy Jack
Russell

I'm little and loveable.

lively little dogs

whiskery terrier

two hairy terriers

cheerful Chihuahua

Find four more little dogs to put on the rug.

bearded basset hound

Big dogs

How many big dogs can you see?

sleepy
St Bernard

fluffy
Canadian
Eskimo
dog

big
boxer dog

curly
coated
retriever

spotted
dalmatian

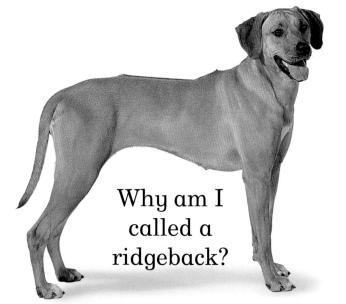
Why am I
called a
ridgeback?

three loveable Labradors

two rugged mountain dogs

hairy sheepdog

rusty red Irish setter

I'm big and cuddly!

Find a tasty dog biscuit for each big dog.

All sorts of dogs

Dogs come in all sorts of
shapes and sizes.
They can be...

...fluffy tailed

...rolled and wrinkly

...very, very
hairy

...smooth
and shiny

...short
and sweet

Have you ever
seen dogs
like these?

Look at my
spotted chest!

We're a furry family.

We're long and loveable.

Find some
more balls
to balance on
the acrobatic
dog's nose.

7

Puppy playtime

Look at all the fun the puppies are having!

Ring, ring, who's there?

Does anyone want to play ball?

I'm going to score a goal!

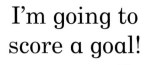

Is it my turn yet?

Time for a hug with bear.

Peek-a-boo!

Stickers

page 3

pages 4 and 5

page 7

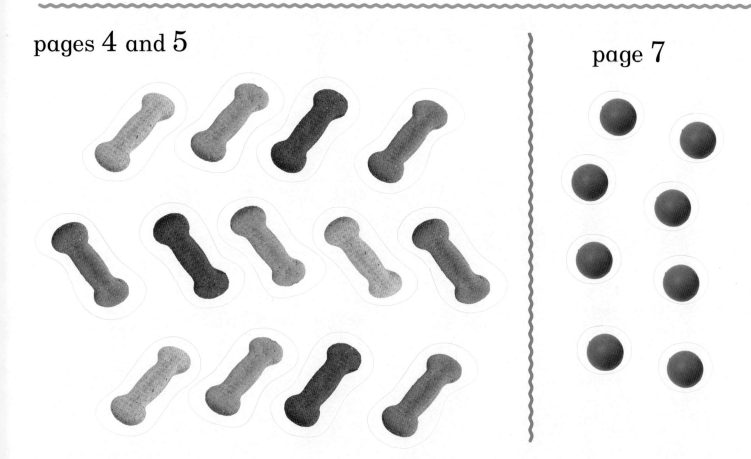

pages 8 and 9

page 11

pages 12 and 13

page 15

Choo, choo, goes the train.

Do you know this tune?

I'm going to catch that frisbee!

This looks interesting.

We're only play fighting!

Can I get in too?

Find some more toys for the dogs to play with.   9

Daydreaming
What are all these dogs daydreaming about?

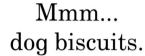

Mmm... dog biscuits.

Yummy... suppertime!

I'd like some dog treats.

My sweetheart.

I'm thirsty. I'd like some water.

Find these doggies' dreams!

I'm winning!

I want a
new car.

What am I
dreaming about?

I want my very
own poodle
salon.

Ahhh...
my new
home.

Dog fashion

These dogs are all dressed up and ready to go!

Bow ties are cool!

Look at my knitted jacket...

...and my trendy overcoat.

elegant evening collar

fabulous golden collar

This is my best sweater.

Find bows and hats for this row of dogs.

12

shiny
sparkling
collar

Look at my
cool shades!

Do you like my
hairstyle?

smart
black
coat

shiny yellow
raincoat

pretty red
collar

Home sweet home

It's time for the dogs
to go home.

Do you like
my flowery
home?

Peek-a-boo!

I can ride
around in
my red
mobile home.

I'm the king
of the castle.

My house
looks like the
Taj Mahal.

How many
dogs are in
this house?

Look at my garden!

It's snug in my basket.

There's lots of room in my big orange house.

We like our cushion.

Find the dogs to put in their houses.

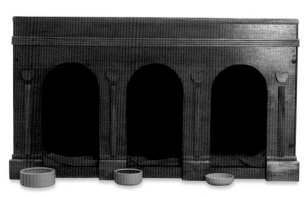

This edition is published by Armadillo,
an imprint of Anness Publishing Ltd

www.annesspublishing.com; twitter: @Anness_Books

If you like the images in this book and would like to investigate
using them for publishing, promotions or advertising, please visit
our website www.practicalpictures.com for more information.

Publisher: Joanna Lorenz
Editors: Jennifer Williams and Richard McGinlay
Special Photography: Jane Burton and John Daniels
Designers: Keith and Clair Watson
Production Controller: Rosanna Anness

The publishers would like to thank the following owners and
breeders for their kind help with the photography: J. Aldrich,
Mr & Mrs M. Beaven, Mrs L. Byles, Carol Cavanagh, D. Chads,
Mrs Cobb, C. Coode, Messrs Cutts & Galvin, J. Ellis, Mrs L. Ellis,
M. Endersby, Mrs J. Farnfield, M. P. & E. Froome, Mrs L. Graham,
M. Gurney, A. Handly, Miss C. Hicks, Mrs S. Hill, K. Holmes &
D. Wisley, Mrs A. Hughes, D. Jenkins, Mrs K. Le Mare, J. Luckett,
Mrs P. Luckhurst, Mrs Mackie, Mrs C. McCutchon-Clarke, Mr & Mrs
D. Miller, Mrs C. Mitchell, L. Powell, Mrs C. Pulbeam, O. A. Sameja,
Mrs E. J. Snowdon, Mrs. G. E. Taylor, Miss S. Taylor, T. Thomas,
R. Tillman, Miss Tonkyn, P. Walden, Mrs R. Welch, A. Wells,
J. White and Mrs R. Wilshaw.

PUBLISHER'S NOTE
The author and publishers have made every effort to ensure that this
book is safe for its intended use, and cannot accept any legal
responsibility or liability for any harm or injury arising from misuse.

Manufacturer: Anness Publishing Ltd, 108 Great Russell Street,
London WC1B 3NA, England
For Product Tracking go to: www.annesspublishing.com/tracking
Batch: 1081-23317-1127